HOPE
BEGINS
AT
HOME

FATHER HARRY BOHAN

CAMPUS PUBLISHING

First published 1993
© Copyright Father Harry Bohan

ISBN 1 873223 01 3

Typeset by Wendy A. Commins
Printed in the Republic of Ireland
by Colour Books Ltd., Dublin 13

Published by
Campus Publishing
26 Tirellan Heights
Galway

Contents

All the rivers run into the sea;
yet the sea is not full;
unto the place from whence the rivers come,
thither they return again.

—Ecclesiastes

Acknowledgements

This book is made up of papers written over a number of years. I do not claim ownership of any original ideas that might be contained in these pages; rather must I acknowledge my debt to the thoughts and words of others whom I do not know and cannot credit individually.

I am very grateful to the people I have worked closely with down through the years. I know they will excuse me for acknowledging the special contribution of Tom Collins of Maynooth—a wonderful academic, and blessed with a huge capacity to be in constant touch with the pragmatists.

Family and friends mean a lot to me: I thank them for their friendship, encouragement and support.

I acknowledge in a special way the contributions of "extra-ordinary" people from the hidden Ireland. In many ways this book is *their* statement although, of course, they cannot be blamed for my personal views.

—H.B.

Introduction

At the outset, let me state that I have a distinct sense of discomfort at putting these few thoughts between covers. This discomfort arises from two sources. Firstly, I admit to an impatience with thought that is not followed by action or informed by action; secondly, my sense of frustration with those forces which are preventing the emergence of the full potential of "ordinary" people to be realised sometimes impedes the cold winds of reason. The ideas presented herein are ones which address such a variety of issues as to risk the accusation of setting oneself up as an expert on a multiplicity of areas.

Despite this discomfort, I am going ahead with publication of this book for one reason: if *Hope Begins at Home* succeeds in generating debate and in challenging the conventional wisdom in Ireland as articulated by dominant forces in our society, then it will have fulfilled my purpose.

I have attempted to present here the major challenges confronting Irish society today, and to point here and there to possible solutions. If I myself am informed by any deep personal belief system, part of it is a fundamental belief in the ability of people to solve their problems, and in the helplessness which occurs when others take it upon themselves to solve these problems for them. A democracy which fails to engage the resources, energy and commitment of people is a democracy which is failing its people. If, in a small country like Ireland, faced as it is with large but very definable problems, we cannot marshal a national commitment towards the solution to these problems, we must begin to examine the basic causes which are preventing this from happening.

Part of this problem in Ireland is the nature of government. Government in Ireland, and the existing state apparatus which supports it, is not only centralised in structure and location but, most importantly of all, is *centralised in attitude*. Hence the problem-solving mechanism in Ireland is one which is more inclined to *exclude* than to *include*, to be *central* rather than *local*; it has a tendency to be contemptuous of the "people-driven" approach.

Having spent my life working in people-centred work I am reminded of Mick Cooley's dictum that he has never met an "ordinary" person—only "extraordinary" ones. I can say, with absolute conviction and humility, that I have spent my life working with extraordinary people. However, these people are on no central stage in Irish society. They are farmers, unemployed men and women, professionals, industrial and office workers, retired people and many others. Many belong to families and to community groups, to associations and to organisations. Many more are people who want to do their "own thing". These people have formed a coherent analysis of their personal situation, invariably with inadequate resources. They are able to run their lives and to solve their own problems, but are prevented from doing so by overbearing forces which insist that only a select few can solve the nation's problems.

My early work with Rural Resource Organisation was informed by a largely instinctive belief that, given resources and some "personal space", individuals throughout rural Ireland could achieve high levels of personal creativity, self-directedness and independence. Indeed, it appeared to me that people started out in life with an innate capacity and drive for self-directedness. The task therefore was less *to create it* than *to release it*.

A systematic policy of diverting national resources away from small communities and away from local endeavour into some grand design has peripheralised rural communities and rural people. At best, it was intended that they would benefit from "trickle-down". At worst, they were simply discarded and disregarded.

Unemployment is probably the best documented indication of marginalisation, but people are also asking what is happening to families, and they are beginning to feel that our system of representative democracy is failing.

My work over the past 20 years has brought me close to these realities. For example, wherever the successes of the past 20 years were being celebrated, I was reminded of failures in so many other places; for every "opening" in one place there was a "closure" elsewhere; for every loudly-acclaimed job created, there was a largely silent loss of a job elsewhere.

And yet despite a long exposure to the frustration of witnessing the social and economic dismembering of a self-sufficient and self-reliant society, I have never lost my complete conviction in the capacity of these "ordinary" people to overcome adversity and to shape rewarding and socially responsible lives.

That our unemployment figures have now reached the 300,000 figure is obviously a serious matter. (Between 1970 and 1990 Ireland's unemployment increased more than threefold.) What is even more serious, however, is the intolerance of the political system to thinking from outside its own small circle. Four decades ago we had developed a capacity in Ireland to accommodate mass emigration. Since 1980 we have been developing a capacity to accommodate mass unemployment. Further, we seem to have replaced any realism in facing up to our situation by continuing to delude ourselves that another array of state machinery, on top of what is already there, is going to solve the problem.

We have had too many over-blown promises, followed by limp excuses for failure. I believe it is important that we begin at least to search for ways to accommodate the "ordinary" people before we are forced to face up to the fateful day. We cannot be too far away from having to confront the dire consequences of mass unemployment and the reality of broken communities, urban and rural.

This could mean exploring every idea other than those which are part of conventional wisdom.

In recent years, I have been much taken by the writing and work of the many "alternative" thinkers, particularly their persuasive arguments against consumerism, against central bureaucratic management and in favour of small-scale locally autonomous production and governmental units. They appear to me to offer hope and a positive view of the future at a time when there is a developing pessimism regarding the potential of the capitalist-industrial grand design.

The future will require, as it always has required, that we confront all problems in new ways or, more likely, new versions of old ways. Even those with the greatest stake in established ways are increasingly recognising the limitations of their approaches. The problem of unemployment and associated problems of social and psychological alienation of large numbers of Irish people have become a matter of great concern.

Throughout Europe there is growing alarm at the emerging unemployment crisis and a recognition that this crisis is no longer confined to the poorer states.

Economic, social and environmental breakdown demand a widening of the parameters of thought, debate and action, creating a greater readiness for change and alternatives. In my own case, I would describe this alternative as one which respects the human need for self-creation, which accords to each person the space and resources to construct his or her life in an energetic and socially responsible way; which is committed to national and global equity and recognises the divinity in mankind and which respects and nurtures all living things.

Hope Begins at Home argues that there is a fundamental redefinition occurring in Irish society. A new vision of the future is being shaped and moulded, and this is happening at the fringes of Irish society rather than at its centre; it is at the bottom rather than at the top; it is more likely to be found in community groups than in universities; amongst women than amongst men, and amongst voluntary groups than in state bodies.

At the risk of over-simplification, the nature of this thinking is one which has a renewed interest in traditional Irish society—in family and community, in spirituality, in roots, in participation, in work, in personal growth, and in the local with a global orientation.

In short, the direction of change is towards people, reclaiming their space, actively owning and producing their own world and, through this, rediscovering meaning, personal identity and purposefulness.

Father Harry Bohan
Shannon, Co. Clare
October, 1993

1. A Personal Journey

I was brought up in a pub in the small village of Feakle in County Clare in the 1940s and 1950s. Anybody brought up in Ireland at that time would have to say that the two institutions that really formed them were the family and the local community. I can certainly say that the family of the 1940s and 1950s had certain obvious features. For example, the traditional farm family or indeed pub family of that time was uncompromisingly dominated by the "boss" in many ways. In other words, all major decisions whether farming, financial or business, were taken by the father. At the same time, the mother had a huge emotional influence on most of the household.

The family was very much a productive unit. As a place of enterprise we all had definite tasks. The males and the females all had different tasks. It was a place that *produced* rather than *consumed*.

The family was very much a place of training and education. In other words, sons grew up learning skills from their fathers. A lot of the character we have came from our parents: we watched what they did and we learned from what they did.

Practically every family felt the influence of other adults, apart from the father and mother. They had grandparents, neighbours, aunts and uncles and close friends. In my own case, I grew up very much with adults because a pub at that time wasn't confined to one room. The pub was part of the kitchen, and part of what you would call today the "sitting-room". People took over the house when they came into the pub in those days.

My family, like other families of the day, were very conscious of their dependence on God. Prayer was important, prayer was necessary and prayer was habitual. It was part of every day. Praying together was vital and togetherness was as important as the prayer, so that the family in that sense had a huge influence in forming me and in forming people of that era.

Feakle in the late 1940s and '50s was a place where families were very self-sufficient. We knew little about government in those times. Feakle was fundamentally a place where people worked hard. There were no hand-outs. People produced their own food and their own fuel. It was subsistence-living; emigration was very much part of it.

Although the family was a huge influence, the wider community also had a major influence on us, mainly through three institutions—the school, the church and the GAA. We were Feakle men and women because of the local parish team. One of the things that kept us going during those years was a great tradition of hurling. The teams of the 1930s and '40s won five championships. They were our heroes. In other words, our heroes were *local heroes*. They weren't from other parts of Ireland and they certainly weren't from across the water.

The Church was a major influence as we came together every Sunday. We came from valleys and hills, and we met after Mass for a chat. Praying in the church was important, but the togetherness of the people after Mass—it was the days of horses-and-carts and asses-and-carts and ponies-and-traps—was very important also.

The children came together in the school. The togetherness was as important to me as the schooling itself. One of the scars that was left on me was seeing my school pals having to emigrate. Nine of the 14 in my class had to emigrate. In fact all 14 of us left the parish. That was a symptom of the kind of place Feakle was. It was a place of great security and great stability, but at the same time of great sadness because of emigration.

My character was shaped and built by seeing my father and mother work hard and making huge sacrifices, so that we could be educated. Secondary school cost money. It may look now like small money, but it was very big money for my parents. They had to make huge sacrifices. I was not the only member of my family going to secondary school. In fact, in a short period of time all four of us were going to secondary schools. I went to St. Flannan's as a boarder, which was obviously more expensive.

My first great wrench in life was having to leave my family and my community. Within a short time, many of my contemporaries left Feakle altogether.

In St. Flannan's, you were expected to be an achiever in sport; you had to be aiming towards "a call" to the Civil Service or to the church. Nobody told us that we should think of going back home. Our education seemed to be directed towards getting us out of where we were and going elsewhere. I think that a lot of emphasis was on the "big job", or the job with status. I would have serious problems today with that kind of education. I would seriously question the role of a secondary school that directed people away from their own localities into other places. Such schools were *in* communities but not *of* them. My abiding memory of St. Flannan's is one of the desperate wrench that I felt every September, every January and every Easter, leaving home.

I didn't feel any inclination towards the priesthood until around the Christmas of my Leaving Cert year. I think that everybody who went through St. Flannan's at least *thought* of going for the priesthood. God permeated all of life in those times, at home, in the community and in Flannan's itself. To try to serve God was a noble ideal but, in addition to that I loved my local community so much that I felt that if I could become a priest and serve in such a place, it would be almost my ideal in life. From a very early stage I felt that helping to hold young people in such communities would be important work. I was at home on holidays, walking along a country road on the night that I decided I was going to be a priest. Mind you, I had several doubts as I went through Maynooth, but from there on I had no doubts that I was what I wanted to be ...

I went to Maynooth in 1956. The first thing Maynooth meant for me was that you met people from other parts of Ireland. Feakle had been my mould until I went to Flannans, where I met people from Tipperary and west Clare. In Maynooth I met people from all over Ireland. I discovered the self-confidence of the young students from the North of Ireland; they certainly seemed to have a lot more confidence than lads like myself.

It was really from the early 1960s onwards that *social questions* became a major one for the church. *Mater et Magistra* was the first and great encyclical of that era, from Pope John XXIII. Jeremiah Newman, who was then the professor of sociology in Maynooth and is now Bishop of Limerick, encouraged us to study sociology, and how theology could be preached and lived in the context of the society of our changing world. He brought us together not only in the formal class situation but also in informal groupings to look at the social issues. He asked me to prepare a discussion paper on *Mater et Magistra* for the students. I felt, as I studied it, that Pope John XXIII must have known the west of Ireland: the encyclical dealt with the problems of industrial society, the uprooting of people, poor housing conditions, the value of agricultural society and of rural society, etc. I got a sense that the church was addressing my own experience and my own feelings.

I will be forever grateful for being in Maynooth. It was a most exciting time in Ireland. Great changes were beginning to take place. The industrial revolution was starting in Ireland. John XXIII was writing for a western world that had experienced the industrial revolution 100 years before. In our context, in the Irish context, it was a very exciting time.

It was also the communications era and the era of Vatican II.

On the day that I was ordained, Bishop Joseph Rogers told me that he was sending me to do a post-graduate course at the University of Wales. What he actually said to me was the diocese was changing and Shannon was going to have a huge influence on that change. Bishop Rogers wanted a priest who would have some understanding of what that change was all about. I was ordained in 1963 and I went to Cardiff in October of that year.

I should emphasise that I have been very fortunate in having Michael Harty as my bishop for the past 25 years. He believes that the gospel cannot be preached in a vacuum, but only in the real world. Bishop Harty's support and encouragement have been invaluable to me.

At Cardiff I did a thesis on the growth of cities in Britain. I examined the movement of people out of Ireland from the Famine days through the second half of the last century into the first half of this century, and the horrific conditions in which they lived in the cities in Britain. Huge numbers suffered and died from diseases like typhoid and cholera in the cities of Britain, because they lived in dreadfully overcrowded conditions. I often felt later that the Irish whom I met in the '60s and '70s in Britain, who longed to come back to Ireland, were products of the kind of conditions that many of their predecessors had experienced in Britain. My studies convinced me that the industrial city was wrong. Creating such overcrowded conditions has to be wrong. I became convinced that I should go back and make some contribution to the Feakles of this world.

The University of Wales was a huge change for me from the enclosed world of Maynooth. An "open" university was a strange but wonderful experience. For example, one of my best friends was a fellow who was living in a derelict house, doing a Ph.D. He is now a lecturer in sociology. He claimed to be a total atheist! I had never met anybody like him before and we became great friends. He used to talk to me about God, and test me about this God that I believed in, which of course was crucial in getting me to examine my faith.

One of my professors was a man called Michael Fogarty, who sometimes asked me to lecture to students on the theology of work. I had never heard of a "theology of work", and this forced me to study the role of God in the world of mammon.

After completing my studies, I was asked to work with the

emigrants in Birmingham. I was broken-hearted leaving Cardiff, but in my two-and-a-half years in Birmingham I came to love the place and the people. I worked in a parish that had 13,000 Catholics. It was the second-biggest parish in England. I was heavily involved in housing and pastoral work. The night before I left Birmingham to come back to Clare, I called to a one-roomed flat where a man and his wife were living with their six children. They were having trouble—the woman had been beaten up by the husband. He asked me if I could do anything for him back in Ireland. "I am sorry for what I did to my wife," he told me. "If you or anyone else were living in those conditions, you would probably do the same thing." I said to myself: "Yes, I probably would." He and other families like his convinced me that something had to be done about families who are uprooted from rural Ireland to live in such conditions. It is very definitely not a recipe for good family living!

I came back to Shannon in the late 1960s. Ireland was alive. Everywhere there was evidence of "progress". People were talking about full employment. It was the Buchanan era—the growth-centre era. I reckoned that we were on a disaster course: to say so, as I did privately and publicly, was at that time almost a mortal sin. What I saw was that we were over-relying on trans-national money. We were putting all our eggs in that basket and were putting all our industry into a few centres. What that meant was that families and local communities were merely suppliers of labour to those growth centres. We were totally neglecting our own natural resources—our sea, our woods, our land—and we were putting billions of pounds into multinational companies. They gave a great service to this country in the 1960s, but it was clear to me that some of those companies would soon be in another part of the world—and that is exactly what happened.

I felt sure that we were facing mass unemployment and urban breakdown. I was so convinced of this—and of the importance of family and community—that I borrowed £1,500 in 1972. I went to a bank manager and told him that, if we could bring young families back to live in the small villages, other things could happen. This was running against the trends of the day.

I owe a lot to that bank manager, Johnny Mee, now retired and living in Galway. Not only did Johnny give me the loan of £1,500, but he agreed to come on a committee with a few other experts to see if we could build 20 houses in Feakle. I said to myself at an early stage: If I cannot do it in Feakle, I can do it nowhere. In Feakle I met the local community and discovered that, in spite of all the progress in the rest of the country, Feakle had only three people between the ages of 20 and 40 in 1972. That spelt disaster. In other words, that village that I grew up in and loved had been written off.

All the experts told us that people would not go back to live in my village. I was told by an expert that we were crazy to do what we were doing, that we would finish up in jail.

The parish priest announced at Sunday Mass that young families who would like to live in Feakle should come to the hall on the following Friday night. This seemed crazy at that time. Families *didn't* come—because they were not there, but their relatives came. Some of them came from Dublin and elsewhere; we got 20 families into the hall on that Friday night. Eventually, through a lot of scraping, bowing, back-breaking, and bringing bags of cement into the site, we got 20 young families back into Feakle. That was *enormous* in a small village population. It probably meant an increase of about 100 people, in the age group which was needed. This convinced me that we were right. We formed a company. Other villages saw our achievement and we moved on from there. Since then, we have built 2,500 houses in 120 communities in 13 counties. The spin-off became obvious very quickly. For example, Con Smith (now gone to God) built a village hotel, which was unheard of—we never had tourists in Feakle. Instead of losing a teacher, the school got an extra one. Young farmers stayed on the land; people began to set up little enterprises. It happened in many other villages as well. All of that activity, by a voluntary organisation, represents an investment of

17

about £200 million in rural Ireland—and by the people themselves.

It was often said to me that I was a romantic, and my idea couldn't work. That was the challenge—we *had* to make it work. I remain convinced that the era of the industrial city is over. There is too much crime and there is too much family breakdown. I also believe that family breakdown itself has come about largely because families have become consumers and not producers.

John Paul II said, when he came to Ireland: "Keep in contact with your roots in the soil of Ireland, with your families and your culture." That is basically what my philosophy is. If you uproot people and break the togetherness of family life and community, then you run the risk of building a society on a narrow form of economics which has failed on three counts. (1) People no longer participate as we did in determining our future. (2) Mass unemployment results and (3) multi-poverty systems emerge.

In many of our urban housing estates today, people don't just suffer from lack of money. They suffer from all kinds of deprivations, although the "rooting" of the family and the "rooting" of the community are crucial for the future of a healthy society.

Prayer energises me and keeps me going. I'm not good at praying: I have to struggle hard to pray. I believe that the Lord Himself is coming alive in modern Ireland and in my life. I love the daily Mass and the Eucharist. Like everyone else, I meet with huge obstacles; at the same time I meet with huge encouragement from extraordinary people. Whether it is the encouragement or the struggle of people with their problems, I thank God that I have been given the opportunity to do this work.

The rest of this book looks at the family and its significance for society. The family, for me and my generation, was the school of enterprise and education, of formation and nurturing. What has been happening to strip it of its functions and to alter its nature?

Returning to the family, the community and to roots could be a strategy western society will have to consider. It makes sense that responsibility is given back to people—to act locally and think globally.

2. Keeping The Family Together

The family as we have come to know it is under threat: make no mistake about it. There is hardly a family in the country that has not been touched in some way by the breakdown in the traditional family unit.

The challenges facing the family are enormous. To survive and prosper, it now needs all the support that can be given from every quarter. The *nature* of that support is crucial: effective support can be fashioned only from real knowledge, from learning from mistakes, from examining the challenges themselves. What *causes* family break-ups? How can society help the family, which is its basic unit? How can the family help itself?

Let's begin by looking at the Irish family unit in three distinct phases of the 20th century.

1. The family of the 1930s, '40s and '50s
2. The family of the 1960s, '70s and '80s
3. The family of the 1990s and onwards.

1. The Family of the 1930s, '40s and '50s

Family life had certain obvious features in these decades.

1. The traditional farm family was uncompromisingly dominated by the "boss": all major decisions, farming and financial, were taken by the father. Sons, even into their middle age, were given little authority and were still referred

to as "the boys". The woman had control over whatever income was gained from such activities as the sale of butter and eggs. She would, however, be free to make decisions about the training and education of children. Among some urban families, this strong authoritarian image seems to have been less in evidence.

2. There were clear sets of male and female tasks and they represented the natural order of things. Arensberg and Kimball wrote in the 1930s: "For a man to concern himself with a woman's work, such as the sale of eggs or the making of butter, is the subject of derisive laughter." (C. Arensberg and S. Kimball: *Family and Community in Ireland*) This was reflected in the training both sexes received from early life—most of the heavy work was done by the man, while the wife dominated all activities within, and to some extent around, the house.

3. Marriages were very often "arranged", legally or otherwise. Often the marriage was an unequal partnership. The typical form of marriage in rural Ireland was the "match". It was seen very much as a social and economic vehicle for survival in a society where physical survival was a constant preoccupation. "Marriage was likely to be contemplated not when a man needed a wife but when the land needed a woman." (K.H. Connell: *Irish Peasant Society*)

4. The family was very much a production unit, an enterprise with clear sets of male and female tasks but within which children played an important part. Smaller children spent time playing; older children did work that was needed around the house—they all had their jobs (drawing water, chopping wood, preparing meals). Older children also worked alongside their parents, sharing in the day-to-day tasks of making the family work: they were involved in a kind of serious apprenticeship, and they often had definite and serious levels of responsibility.

5. Practically every family had other adults, apart from the mother and father, associated with it—grandparents, unmarried uncles, aunts, hired help, neighbours and close friends of family. Recreation centred around talk with them. Children listened: a big threshold was crossed when older children were welcomed into this circle of discussion.

6. The whole family was conscious of their dependence on God. Prayer was important, necessary and habitual. *Praying together* was vital and the togetherness was as important as the prayer.

We should not over-romanticise this bygone era, but I think we should note that the role of the family was clear, that parental influence was strong, that from an early age people were involved in necessary work and so a sense of responsibility and a sense of worth were conveyed. A lot of learning was done within the home: young and old shared work, prayer and leisure. Because future occupational positions were more or less fixed, parents thought more of their children's future *character* than of their *careers*: will they be honest, level-headed, honourable? Will they bring esteem to the family? Can we count on them to respect us in our old age?

2. The Family of the 1960s, '70s and '80s

The roots of change go back to the promise of personal freedom which began to replace the notion of "duty" in the second half of this century. Two broad developments brought this about.

(a) First is the unprecedented and ever-growing level of prosperity. In a real sense, we have all acquired material benefits undreamed of by those who went before us. The growth of industry and complex urban life changed things radically. The family has become very much more a consumer of goods rather than a producer.

21

(b) The second is the rise of mass electronic communications which has introduced powerful images, ideas, values and authority figures.

We will look at the implications of these but first we should note a few other clearcut changes in the structure of the family:

- There is a definite pattern in the decline of the large three-generational household.

- The position of the elderly has altered radically with the decline of the extended household: in the past, the "boss" tended to hold on to control and ownership of the farm until well into old age. "They live long because they have much to live for. In their own sphere of life, they are honoured, they have power."

- The number of single-parent families is a definite phenomenon. In 1980 the nuclear family accounted for only 45% of all households; single persons account for 17% and alone parents 9%. If patterns in other industrialised societies are to be repeated here, the single-parent family is likely to become second only to the nuclear family as the dominant family unit.

Let us briefly look at how these social changes have affected the woman, the father, the children.

Woman

The dream of freedom touched the life of woman most deeply. It offered her a greater sense of security, raising her self-image. She grew from being a subservient human being to a *person* with the right to choose her own destiny. She questioned her traditional role in the family: she challenged the "arranging" of marriages, and the legal and political inequality that made her a minor for her entire life. As tame as it may sound, the concept of a freely chosen marriage was not only revolutionary in itself but it put a premium on personal freedom and individual conscience, as well as on shared responsibility to protect those values.

Society is since out of breath, trying to keep up with the revolution she began. It was woman as person, armed with freedom made possible by technology, that changed the family of the '30s, '40s and '50s and has created the family of the '70s, '80s and '90s. For this reason most books on parenting or childcare have tended to emphasise the mother-child relationship in children's upbringing. I suppose it is true to say that these revolutionary concepts of *woman as person* and *marriage as partnership* challenge the family in a number of ways but certainly on three important levels—children, career, permanence.

Children: A common birth rate pattern began to emerge in the west, despite differences of religion, economic policies or legislation that encourages or discourages large families. Simply put, couples rarely wanted more than two children on average and they wanted them after the fifth year of marriage.

Career: With the philosophy of marriage as an equal partnership, better education, fewer children to care for, financial pressures, more and more women are taking a career outside the home. The nature of work itself, with an increase in intellectual occupations and light industrial work, has changed in a way which works in women's favour. Women were always an important part of the work force, but what is new is that the number of women working outside the home has increased because many more skilled jobs have been opened to them. The era of the dual career family is with us.

Permanence: When young couples decide to marry today, they will probably have to work at it for 50 years on the average. In the '50s, Ireland had the lowest marriage rate in Europe and very high celibacy rates—1 in 4 women and 1 in 3 men aged 55-plus were unmarried. The average marriage age was 33 for men and 28 for women. Marriage became more popular in the '60s and '70s and the average age for marriage dropped: in 1980 it was 27 years for men and 24 years for women. If one accepts the greater scope of personal freedom and individual conscience as a sign of progress, then it must be accepted that a modern marriage makes great demands on a relationship.

Statistics from other countries show that failure in marriage is a growing probability. The total number of divorces in the EC countries increased from 125,000 in 1960 to 421,000 in 1980.

In the United Kingdom, during that period, the number of divorces increased from 25,900 to 159,700. In Ireland, of course, the State is prohibited from enacting any law which provides for the grant of a dissolution of marriage. What is permitted is a judicial separation of partners but this does not allow re-marriage of separated partners and, of course, the Church would not recognise any decree of dissolution granted by the State. It should be noted too that the growth in the divorce rate elsewhere has generally been accompanied by a dramatic rise in the number of re-marriages. The relationship between divorce and the instability of family life is complex. One can ask: does the growing instability of the family lead to a liberalisation of divorce laws or *vice versa*?

Although marriage appears, at least outwardly, to be the outcome of individual choice in modern society, some controls over marriage are exercised by individuals or groups other than the partners. Among the most important of these are age, kinship, religion, property, social class.

The Father
In recent times, people studying changes in family life and family influences have reported a connection between the erosion of the father's influence and the emergence of young people from childhood with problems deriving from weakness of character, immaturity and irresponsibility, alcohol and drug abuse, religious indifference, marital instability, separation.

Let us then try to see the effect some of these changes have had on the family with particular emphasis on the father.

1. Children today almost never see their father at work: he leaves in the morning and arrives home tired at night. They do not see him exercising his personal powers of mind, or

the skill and strength of his hands; they do not observe him exercising his character in action on the job. When they do see him at home they generally see him at leisure—even if he does jobs around the house, it is usually a leisure activity, a break from the pressures of his serious livelihood. Children rarely work now with their father. Increasingly, the children do not see the mother at work either. Pressures for a second income and for material things—mortgages, etc.—now keep Mom also out of the house. So her own example as personal provider, with on-the-job skills, is diminished considerably. Many children see their parents mostly at rest and most especially in front of the television. Unfortunately, serious strengths of character do not normally shine forth in leisurely amusements, and certainly not in front of the television.

2. The home itself has become a place of play rather than work. Tools and work implements once abounded in the home and toys and playthings were scarce: today the situation is reversed. Playthings are very obvious in the home—television sets, radios, stereos, videos, table games, pooltables, boxes of toys and so on. Typically, books are scarce. A visitor from the '40s and '50s would notice the role-reversal in the family. In those times, the children shared in adult activities. Now the parents are given over to the children's preoccupations, which is principally amusement.

3. Conversation with the father and other adults is minimal. If a parent, particularly a father, spent much time talking with his children about his life outside their experience—his job and his life growing up, his concerns and worries, his opinions and convictions—he could compensate considerably for his absence during most of the children's waking hours. The children would learn, at least, something about his character. Apparently this kind of conversation is rare: again, it goes back to things like the television set. It is now said by professionals who work with troubled young adults and

adolescents that a striking trait these young people have in common is they know very little about their fathers and they have little or no respect for them.

If conversation with parents is minimal, communication with other adults can be more sketchy: grandparents and other close relatives, for example, often live at some distance from the home. Neighbours are at best only superficial acquaintances and relations with teachers and clergy might be fairly fleeting. Children can grow up today without a range of real-life grown-ups who can serve to round out their concept of adulthood; it can happen that the only other source from which to form a vision of normal adult life is the television.

This isolation contrasts with the adolescent's social circumstances. Every day at school, for example, teenagers have contact with a lot of their peers and obviously they can easily identify with teen culture which can give support to aggressive defiance at home. In that context, many parents find themselves today almost in the position of being out-numbered. It is worth noting here also that people in sport can have a fairly significant influence on young adults now. For example, coaches and trainers of teams might be the only adult males whom children witness close up in the act of working. Coaches and people in sport today can actively help to form character in young people, building personal strengths of mind and will and so on. You will hear many people today expressing their gratitude and respect for people in sport who helped them so much in boyhood.

4. Other children and adolescents today function as consumers not producers. In most reasonably well-off middle-class families, the children's active labour is not really necessary. Many parents find it easier in the long run to do the chores themselves rather than to ask the children. Of course, it is true also that families in poorer circumstances and bigger families have a real need for the children's contributions. Relative

poverty means added work, as it always has, and this leads to real responsibility.

Youngsters in middle-class families are much more consumers of goods and services. Having plenty of time, disposable income and a lot of exciting new interests, these young people constitute a substantial market for commercial exploitation. Often, when given an opportunity to do part-time jobs or get involved in social service or voluntary work, these people can be quite eager in that involvement. They have a chance to prove themselves; in a sense, they are looking for respect. I believe this is something we should encourage. If we don't, a lot of young adults can arrive at their twenties with almost no experience of productive, satisfying work. Instead, a lot of their experience would be centred around leisure activity and so it is no wonder they come to equate happiness with amusement.

5. Television and other entertainment media have become the principal means by which children form concepts of adult life. The rise of television as an authority figure has been one of the most subtle and significant social changes of the past several decades. Its effects are only now beginning to be appreciated. Television presents children with an array of authoritative adult figures—rock singers, musicians, actors, actresses, chat show hosts, etc. Many children know more about these people than they do about their grandparents.

The key point is: these people radiate a power that over-shadows the children's perception of their parents' strengths of character.

When second and third level students are asked which people they most admire, the result is an odd mixture of personalities: Mother Teresa, Pope John Paul II, one or two prominent political figures, and then a collection of names from the entertainment world. What have all these people in common? Simply that they all appear frequently on television. Professional entertainers exercise a direct effect on the way

27

young people talk, think, dress and behave. It is true, I think, that young people seldom talk seriously about any profession other than entertainment. When they do discuss other lines of work (law, medicine, business, etc.) their concepts reflect largely what they have seen dramatised on television.

6. Finally, I suppose it is true to say that the period of prosperity in the '60s and '70s tended to crowd out some of the central realities of life: that we are all totally dependent on God, and that we answer to Him for the way we live. Prosperity gives us the illusion that we have life under control, and wealth's power diminishes our sense of ultimate responsibility. This growth of prosperity and other things meant significantly less family prayer. This in turn meant that many children hardly ever experienced prayer in their lives at home.

    It would seem crucially important for young children to see their parents showing affection and respect for God. By their attitude and actions, parents, in effect, demonstrate that this is the correct way by which we adults regulate our lives and world. Religious conviction has to be one of the greatest strengths in a person's life. It leads to many other personal strengths as well.

Some characteristics of this second phase of family life which we might note are:

• The historic triumph of secularism and individualism has presented a set of problems that is now beginning to loom large for us. Release from traditional ties of class, religion, and kinship has given us freedom but not in a creative sense: we have become more dependent on outside organisations, such as the state, and increasingly disenchanted and alienated.

3. The Family of the 1990s

What sort of family are we going to have, in this last decade of the 20th century?

I see the family as a community, people linked together by close ties and by common purpose. A healthy family is one in which the members *grow together*. These for me are the crucial elements—there is growth, there is togetherness and there is a growing together.

In what way does modern social and economic life allow for growing together? Sadly, our structures do precisely the opposite. Living as I do in Shannon, the image of the family as an airport suggests itself. Airports are characterised by people in motion: they are coming and they are going. The only significance which the airport has is as a distribution point to the different destinations. The modern family is a bit like that. Mornings are characterised by frenetic activity as the members prepare to depart for the day. The members will spend the main part of the day out of each others' company. Mothers, fathers, children all have separate agendas and separate locals. As evening draws in, the members return: the evening meal is now the main event, if not the only family event, of the day. On its completion, the demands of leisure or study or whatever are likely to split the family once again.

While the members of this unit may sleep under the one roof, it is difficult to say that they actually live under it. Where is the common purpose and shared agenda in this unit?

If family life is to be revitalised, we must be clearer about the objectives of family life and about the external structures which will enable us to meet these objectives.

My objective for family life would be one which would see the members involved with one another in the essential components of their lives, particularly in the areas of wealth-creation, education, prayer, formation and leisure. Without shared purpose or shared activity, the spiritual and emotional experience of the family will suffer. *Prayer is as much about being together as it is about praying.* This is the joy of family life and also its meaning.

This, no doubt, leaves me open to accusations of romanticising or idealising family life. Where are the possibilities of togetherness in today's world?

Generally, our broader social structures do not facilitate such togetherness. However, even as things stand, there are more opportunities than we are availing of, and more people are making choices in this direction. A lot of schooling could go on in the home, or in a small local setting run by parents not working outside the home. Much of the leisure industry could become family-oriented, rather than individual-oriented. A lot of work now carried out in offices and factories could be done in the home. We have entered the age of the computer: could this bring many experiences back to the house?

The main impact of the industrial revolution on family life was that the family lost its productive function. Production and consumption became split, with production moving to the factories and workers having to follow it. Producers became employees.

Family life today is denied this possibility. The family is reduced to little more than a depot.

Within this scenario, what is surely remarkable about families is not so much why so many break up as why so many stay together.

Through the ages, communities have recognised the emotional and spiritual value of shared work. Monastic communities were built around it. Even in industrial societies, one can still find examples of shared community-based work—the mining industry in Yorkshire, for example, where generation followed generation into the mines.

Here at home, we are beginning to see the re-emergence of the community in many other areas, now that the larger political organisations and bureaucracies are seen to have failed. We have seen the creation of community watch, community colleges, community health care, community hospitals—people are beginning to see that we will have to return to the community and family if jobs are to be created. Provision of other services could see us return to the community. There is a realisation afoot that, while we are constantly trying to make democracy work, it cannot happen without the allegiances of smaller internal units of family, local community and associations of people. These are the units that contain the images of the larger society, within which human beings are able to define meaningful, democratic values.

I see the whole pastoral thrust emerging *within the Church* as one of building community, based on the family and on groups of families. Pastoral visitation would take the form of the priest and others visiting homes—but with a definite purpose: to facilitate people to cross thresholds next door and down the road. A recreation of the old Station Mass seems to have a value: within the old but eternal Word lie the seeds of survival and prosperity for the family.

I am suggesting, therefore, that the family has an enormously important role to play, but has been experiencing great change. What *are* the vital functions performed by the family?

3. The Family As School

As was pointed out in the previous chapter, a great many changes have taken place in Irish society in the last quarter of a century, leading to a new uncertainty and insecurity in life.

Against this background of rapid change, people would have looked to the Church as the one stable element in their lives. Here also there has been change, and it has come about within a couple of decades after about 400 years of comparative unchange. Because of this it has come as a greater shock. The obvious changes that have taken place are in the liturgy—language, participation of lay people, etc.

Rapid change is, therefore, a comparatively new phenomenon. Well-tried beliefs and units of society are put to the test and sometimes undermined. Traditionally, as we have seen, an outstanding feature of Irish life has been the peculiar relationship between family and community.

Down through history we find that the primary social unit is, in fact, a group of families, living and working together (developed out of the extended family), addressing itself to the task of survival. This has been the pattern until recent times. It has taken various forms at different times—the extended family, the village, the small market town with its hinterland, the cluster of neighbourhoods making up the human city with its pedestrian centre. Not until we come to modern society do we find the isolated nuclear family as it exists today. Suburbanisation and massive housing estates have been the major phenomena of "settlement" growth.

There is no doubt that the nuclear family (parents and their immediate children) is probably more isolated and vulnerable than ever before in the history of man. As western society has emerged, we seem to be left with, on the one hand, the isolated nuclear family and, on the other, the state (with government departments growing everywhere) and the multi-nationals, the giant corporations, financial institutions and organisations with sectional interests.

The isolated family seems to have no choice but to concede some of its essential functions to one or other of these impersonal state, commercial or professional organisations. This is the real struggle which has been going on during our time—not the apparent battles between right and left, between socialism and capitalism, between church and state, but the relentless transfer of power and control from the basic units of society to large bodies and organisations, from the personal to the anonymous and institutional. This change will have to be seriously examined if catastrophe is to be avoided. What then is the role of the family in Irish society?

"Pillar of Society"

The statement that the family is the "pillar of society" has become something of a cliché. Unfortunately, it is a phrase that we seem to use only in the context of pointing out the evils of divorce, abortion, contraception. I want to look at that phrase, not as an argument *for* or *against* anything, but in itself, in order to bring out something of what it really means. I want to try to suggest how the role of the family should be seen in society and in the church, and to analyse what it is that the family contributes to *human*, *social* and *religious* development.

These three forms of development can take place only in the context of personal relationships. The most fundamental answer to a person's need for companionship and sharing and community is the relationship of man and woman, on which the family is founded. Marriage is or should be the most intimate and enriching of personal relationships.

33

School of Human Living

It is in the context of this basic relationship that the human child is born. Without such a context, the process of passing on human life would be incomplete. Birth is only the beginning. For the parents, it is an undertaking, a responsibility. The Second Vatican Council says: "Since parents have conferred life on their children, they have a most solemn obligation to educate their off-spring." The new-born child is a human person, but it is not yet able to function in a human way—not just in the obvious sense of being unable to provide himself or herself with food and shelter, but in the sense of being incapable of speaking, of understanding and participating in human society, incapable even of coming to a basic outlook on the world that will allow him to live in a rational, intelligent manner. All this the child acquires in the family relationship. If one is to have a positive regard for oneself, then one must feel accepted by others.

The family is the setting which provides this essential sense of being accepted. "Home," as Robert Frost put it, "is the place where, when you go there, they have to take you in." Without some such base on which to build, a person would never be able to view other people except as threats to himself or herself.

Not only does the family provide the child with that sense of being loved and accepted which makes human growth possible, it also provides him with close experience of the relationship between parents. In the happy family a child grows to awareness of his surroundings in the closest contact with an instance of what people can mean to each other, how they can trust one another, how "I" and "you" can become "we".

It is not only the children who benefit. Marriage is a growth of the couple themselves. Because it is life lived at close quarters, it carries with it the possibility of becoming a hell, but it also has the potential to become an incomparable growth in communion between two people in which each calls for the best in the other.

The family is a whole network of relationships: the traffic is not all one way. The parents help each other and they help their children. It is also true that children are a source of human growth for the parents. The generosity that is called for, especially by the young child, is a lesson in the meaning of love.

This parental role is almost irreplaceable. To say this may seem disheartening to those who are trying to raise children in institutions, or are trying to compensate for the failures of inadequate parents. But I am simply pointing out something which all these dedicated people know very well—that they are trying to fill a gap, especially on the emotional level. They are trying to provide a child with the things that a healthy family *would* provide. Their aim is to supply, as far as possible, the love of a father and mother; the headline which guides them is their vision of what family life should be. Of course, it is difficult, but it is also, perhaps, the most basic of all forms of Christian concern and social action.

School of Social Living

What I have been saying up to this refers, for the most part, to the ideal or, at least, the satisfactory family. If that situation changes radically, then a great deal of remedial social action becomes necessary. However, the family is "the pillar of society" in a more pervasive sense. The Vatican Council calls it "the first and vital cell of society". If this cell functions in a reasonably healthy manner, the members of the family are able to play a positive role in the wider society. Even the most basic social attitudes and abilities are first acquired in the family—the ability to speak and communicate with others, the experience of living with other people in an atmosphere of mutual acceptance, the sense of fairness and justice in the treatment of others. The family is the first community, the group in which the child learns to say, *and mean*, what is perhaps the most important of all words—"we".

Social living requires that a person should give to others within the community something of the loyalty and sense of respect and responsibility that he owes to his own family. It is interesting to note that the word we use to describe full and constructive community living is a family word, *brotherhood* or *sisterhood*. The fact that a healthy family life equips people to live in society and with the ability to co-operate with others is not an accidental bonus. Part of the essence of a good family is to be outward looking.

This is an aspect about which we have not thought sufficiently. We have always seen that one function of the Christian family is to equip its members to be good citizens. "Especially by example (parents) should teach (children) little by little to show concern for the material and spiritual needs of their neighbour. The whole of family life, then, would become a sort of apprenticeship for the apostolate. Children must … be educated to transcend the family circle." (*Decree on the Apostolate of the Laity*)

The Council documents also insist that the family has an important social role. This is recognised by everybody in the matter of adoption and fostering. It must go further than that. The Council suggests that it should extend to "hospitality to strangers, assistance in the operation of schools, helpful advice and material assistance for adolescents, help to engaged couples in preparing themselves better for marriage, cathechetical work, support of married couples and families involved in material and moral crises, help for the aged".

It may be here that many of the human problems can best be tackled. Making such family involvement a reality is not, I think, a matter of vast and complex organisations; rather, it means bringing home to individual families and groups of families their potential, their competence and their responsibility. Maybe here there should be much more support for family life, emphasising this particular role as well as others rather than so much interest in social service organisations, etc.

One way of underlining the role of the family as the school of social living is to see to what extent a family is really society in miniature. Many of the underlying tensions of society are, first of all, *family problems*. Most obviously of all, there is the problem of the generation gap. A family, by definition, is a generation gap, with all the difficulties and all the potential enrichment that this implies. Society grows, not by a deadening sameness about its members, but by the harmonising and reconciliation of differences. This is something that begins in the family, in the differences in attitude and outlook between parents and children. Again the Vatican Council taught us: "In (the family) the various generations come together and help one another to grow wiser and to harmonise personal rights with the other requirements of social life." (*Constitution on the Church in the Modern World*, Paragraph 5, 2)

Parents inject an element of realism and caution into the idealism and enthusiasm of their children; it is to be hoped that parents in turn catch something of the idealism and enthusiasm that they may be in danger of losing and that their minds may be open to issues and attitudes that they might not otherwise meet.

It is in the family that one first meets the problem which is the most basic social problem of all—how to reconcile the needs and desires of the individual with the good of the group. Children learn that they cannot have every toy, record or holiday that they might like; they gradually come to see that parents are limited by financial realities and by their recognition of the needs of the rest of the family. The important thing is that this happens in an atmosphere of love, so that, as the child throws a tantrum and says, "You're mean!", he knows deep down that this is not true. The problem of the distribution of the resources of society is argued on the same basis as the need to be fair in the family.

"How would you like it if somebody did that to you?"

"I was there first!"

"But you promised!"

"Why can't I just have it for a minute, you're not using it?"

These are the attitudes that grow into what, in the larger context, is more elegantly called a "social conscience".

It is in the family, too, that we meet the problem of the relationship between authority and individual responsibility. Parents have the very difficult task of providing for and encouraging their children, while remaining aware that the proper line of development and choice of career for this child may be very different from what they imagined. They may fondly imagine or, worse still, say that "he or she will be a doctor, or teacher or social scientist like Mummy or Daddy", running the risk of seriously misdirecting a young life, since the daughter or son may be a budding artist or missionary. Authority is a service which is aimed at allowing people to be themselves, to develop along the path that is best for them. Unfortunately, the lessons learned about the exercise of authority as a parent can be difficult to apply successfully in the wider sphere of the "rat race" situation. Nevertheless, I suspect that they are the fundamental lessons— co-operation, tolerance, trust and the recognition that those who exercise authority and those who are subject to it are engaged in a common task and that their interests ultimately coincide.

School of Christian Living

If the home is the place where the child begins to live humanly and socially, it is also where life begins as a Christian. "The family is, so to speak, the domestic church. In it, parents should, by their word and example, be the first preachers of their faith to their children." (*Constitution on the Church*, Paragraph 11) Parents preach the faith not only by what they say, by their example of religious practice and prayers but, much more fundamentally, by what they *are*. "God created man in his own image, in the image of God he created him; male and female he created them." (*Genesis* 1:27)

Married love is the first image of God which we encounter. There is no use in talking about God as a father to a person who has no experience of what fatherhood can mean. A teacher of religion will have difficulty in talking about a good God as a "father" if the word "father" means violence and drunkenness and intolerance to the child. It is in the good home that we learn

38

and live the ideas which make it possible to love God—not just parenthood but love, loyalty, generosity and truth. How can the constant, unwavering character of God's love be communicated to a person who experiences hate between man and woman in a family setting?

The language of religion, like language in general, is learned in the home: these words will always carry the overtones which they acquired in the family. This is the most basic reason why parents are the primary religious educators of their children— their love for one another and for their children is the experience on which our ability to relate to all others, even God, is based. Their love is our first introduction to the very idea of love. They are the first religious educators because, as the Council puts it, by virtue of the fact of being parents they are "co-operators with the love of God, the Creator and are, so to speak, the interpreters of that love". (*Constitution on the Church in the Modern World*, Paragraph 50)

In the Epistle to the Ephesians, St. Paul shows that Christ must be understood in the light of married love, just as marriage must be understood in the light of Christ. "Husbands, love your wives, as Christ loved the Church and gave himself up for her ... that he might present the church to himself in splendour, without spot or wrinkle or any such thing, that she might be holy and without blemish." (*Ephesians* 5:25/27)

The sort of relationship that exists in a happy family may seem to be an unattainable ideal for society as a whole. In a Christian perspective that ideal is not unattainable—it is the Kingdom of God. Our destiny of fulfilment is presented in the imagery of home and marriage: "I saw the Holy City, and the new Jerusalem, coming down from God out of heaven, as beautiful as a new bride all dressed for her husband ... here God lives among men. He will make His home among them; they shall be His people and He will be their God ... He will wipe away all tears from their eyes; there will be no more death, and no more mourning or sadness. The world of the past is gone." (*Revelations* 21:2-4)

The Root of Church and State

The family is therefore the root of both church and state. It is the primary instance of the sort of relationship on which society is built; at the same time, it is the fundamental human sharing in the divine love of which the Kingdom of God consists.

The three aspects of this that I have been talking about—that the family is the source of the individual's ability to live humanly, of social living, and of Christian living—are summed up as follows: "The wellbeing of the individual person, of human and Christian society, is intimately linked with the healthy condition of that community produced by marriage and family." (*Constitution on the Church in the Modern World*, Paragraph 4:7)

To tackle social or religious problems at their root very frequently means tackling them in the family. Violence and aggression, inability to relate to others, lack of trust, are the root of many social problems. While not under-valuing the essential and dedicated work that tries to cure the symptoms of these attitudes, surely we must find some more successful means of preventing at least some of these tragedies from arising by helping families to be what they could and should be?

Above all, it may be important to consider the help that families can give not just to their own members but to society as a whole. The family as an agent of social healing is a force that we have not sufficiently tapped. In all three areas—human, social and Christian living—there are wider and more adventurous possibilities that hold great promise from within the family.

Members of all families undergo the experience of school, which obviously plays an important part in all our lives. Does the experience of school now contribute to strengthening family and community life, or could it have assumed roles which do not belong to it? Is school *in* communities or merely *of* them?

I will be suggesting that school will have to take a radical shift in direction if it is to make sense to people in years to come.

4. The Work Of Schools

Those of us who have been involved with the family and family enterprises—trying to develop local resources, revitalise local communities, identifying with local initiatives—have seen government and its agencies pursue strategies since about 1970 which have been a dismal failure. These strategies totally ignored the people themselves and their local resources, whose development was left to voluntary bodies and individuals who work in the backyard of reality. The social effects of this misguided policy—unemployment, crime and homelessness— have the horrific proportions of an epidemic, as represented by three distinct groups which have been dispossessed: our poor and unemployed, our emigrants, and the people of broken urban and rural communities.

The plethora of government development agencies which were set up in the early 1960s to solve a particular problem *have now become the problem*. They created a big-firm, big-city, big-institution culture in the 1960s, supported by Irish tax-payers' money. They totally ignored our own Irish resources, both human and material. When "bigness" ceased to create jobs, in the early 1970s, the mind-management and fundamental dishonesty continued. The lack of commitment to local resources is evident. Obvious examples can be found in the sharp contrast between the potholed roads of rural Ireland and the no-expense-spared foreign industry zones, with their attractive buildings, landscaped green areas and brightly coloured signs.

Thus the idea is reinforced that local equals insignificant

equals small-time equals not-worth-while. This brings with it an erosion of people's self-esteem and belief in their capacity for independent and significant action in determining their own future.

To me it is very clear that the reasons for our continual economic regression have more to do with politics and politicians, development agencies and globe-trotters, than with natural resources. We have an abundance of such resources in the form of timber, food, fish, etc. Our people have a great capacity at local level to respond to enterprise possibilities.

All of which leads to the inevitable question: why have these resources and energies been largely ignored by our established development agencies? These agencies have monopolised development over the past 30 years, taking over from individuals, families and whole communities—placing obstacles, deliberate and accidental, in the way of local people attempting to realise their potential.

We need to restore *people* to the centre of the development stage, allowing large agencies a less visible role.

And obviously our schools and universities have a vital role to play in this process of shaping us as individuals, members of families and communities.

Education as we know it today in Ireland evolved largely as a result of the industrial revolution at the end of the 1950s and early 1960s. The needs of the industrial society necessitated a highly skilled workforce. The emergence of a highly developed service sector required an expansion of professional, academic-type education. It *followed* rather than *led*.

Our educational system developed to meet the needs of an economy that seemed to have an insatiable demand for a highly-skilled, highly-educated workforce. A well-educated young person was assured of a place in the economy on leaving school. The content of what the student learned was not too important. School had value and meaning in that it determined the student's life-chances.

For the students of many post-primary schools, therefore, the prospect of unemployment was unlikely. Most students would have shown a clear preference for white-collar work.

Good examination results were the only requirement in this type of system. The better the results, the better the student's place in the economic system afterwards. The teacher's responsibility was to provide the information and stimulation to ensure that each student maximised his or her results.

The problem with this system was that schools not only *followed* but they followed a *once-off investment of money and technology in the 1960s.* They basically followed a materialistic system of bringing about economic growth and social development. When this system no longer proved suitable, there was a vacuum. The education system continues to persist with these patterns, even though the relationship with the economy has totally altered. Nowadays an expanding economy does not necessarily generate a demand for labour as in the past. The contracting labour market has affected not just the manufacturing workforce but also the service sector—banks, insurance companies and so on. Schools therefore can no longer work on the assumption that good results mean a job. Rather they must take cognisance of the widening gap between education and the economy and act on this.

The main task of our educationalists is to equip students for the changed world they are entering. Performing this task now is considerably different to what was involved 20 or 30 years ago. It seems to me that the main attribute which a student should have today on leaving school is a personal capacity to rely on his or her own talents and potential. A sense of self-reliance rather than dependency is now a priority if schools are to realise their obligation to their students.

This brings me to the whole concept of education by, among others, religious and its links with the local community. If, for example, the education system is to become student-centred then it must preoccupy itself with the environment and the community in which its students reside. Second-level schools and third-level institutions in Ireland have mainly seen the community as simply the locality which supplies their students. They have functioned in something of a leech-like manner, drawing away the brighter students out of their local communities and depriving local areas of their own people's talents and resources.

While second-level students, therefore, have been *in* communities they have rarely, if ever, been *of* communities. The main service they have provided to the communities in which they are located is to channel the brightest students out of such communities.

One or two other points, I think, which need to be made here are:

1. It has always seemed to me to be a strange anomaly that educational institutions within the same town are sometimes seen as competing for students, rivals on the examination treadmill. This situation has improved, but there seems to be no organ to bring together, for the avoidance of over-lapping or even for consultation, different educational authorities which have common general interests. Primary education does not seem to be properly co-ordinated with the post-primary system. Despite recent developments, there is still room for improved coordination between the secondary and vocational sectors.

2. Agriculture is our greatest natural resource, but it is scandalously under-developed. Our educational system has shared in the neglect.

    This neglect must be regarded as highly unfortunate in a country which is so dependent on agriculture and which has to compete with countries whose inhabitants are instructed in the most modern methods. For example, there are approximately 30,000 people training in FÁS centres around the country but only 1,000 people are being trained in agricultural science. The under-developed state of agriculture, forests,

44

waters, may be attributed to the fact that agricultural science is not generally taught. Why do schools which look out on the Atlantic Ocean not teach mariculture? What about the huge possibilities of timber processing? Have these no place in our education and training system?

3. The post-primary school system does not seem to be fostering a sense of place, a sense of belonging, an awareness of what is all around us and is obvious. A re-orientation by schools towards the community will have to emphasise an appreciation of community resources and an emphasis on their development.

    Environmental and ecological studies do not form a significant part of the post-primary curriculum, even though most will agree that an appreciation of one's environment is a legitimate educational aim. How many students have been helped to an awareness of their local community—number of farmers, types of enterprises and so on? Could the teaching of geography include a thorough examination of the local area? Does social and political history outline the evolution of government and government agencies and their relevance to the citizen in the community?

I believe that the most fundamental service schooling offers to young people is to help them to think, especially about what is obvious and all around them. Perhaps our educators need to examine whether they are properly equipped to handle this side of schooling.

Failing this, young people will begin to question what they are doing at school and may well opt out. Many more will simply "go to college" because they cannot think of anything else to do. (A great number of these seem to opt for arts courses, which is an issue that ought to be addressed by the universities.)

The fact is that our young people ought not to be directed by their education away from their local resources, away from production to become mere consumers in other places.

5. Helping Ourselves

In this chapter I want to consider further what has been happening to undermine the people's part in their own development and in shaping their own future.

I see the story of indigenous development in Ireland as having three parts:

- The past—which is depressing
- The present—which is a challenge
- The future—which can be very bright

The Past

The story of indigenous development in Ireland goes back a long way. Up to the late 1950s there was no other kind of development except short-lived efforts, because indigenous development had not been taken seriously in the previous 30 years in Ireland by governments or by development agencies. This part of the story is harrowing because the lack of a serious and committed approach to indigenous development has been a huge factor in the growth of the largest queue in Europe—the queue of almost 300,000 non-productive, non-working lives in Ireland today.

Over 40,000 Irish men and women emigrated between 1951 and 1961. This was an enormous haemorrhage for such a sparsely populated country. The flight from the land and emigration brought Ireland to the verge of national destitution. (Incidentally, unemployment reached a record 78,000 in 1957.)

With the First Programme for Economic Expansion in 1958, economic planning became a reality and industrialisation and urbanisation were to give direction to Irish society. The inflow of foreign money and technology was to replace the outflow of people. Full employment was promised.

There was huge success in the early 1960s. From about the middle of the decade, however, the euphoria of the early '60s began to dissipate. This was not acknowledged then and it took the best part of over 20 years for agencies that were put in place in the early '60s to acknowledge that anything had gone wrong.

In the 1970s there was a growing realisation by the people that the quick solutions of the 1960s were not, in fact, solutions at all. Indeed, many of our problems stemmed from there in that they gave rise to a depressing era which probably makes the 1960s look better than they really were.

The argument used in the '60s went something like this:

- Rapid economic development is necessary to achieve personal incomes, better social facilities, more exports, job creation and an end to emigration.
- All this can be achieved through rapid industrialisation.
- This requires concentration in a few major centres.

The argument had some validity but some major problems accompanied it. I would just like to touch on three of these.

1. Demoralisation of rural communities: these places which had all the natural resources were seen simply as suppliers of labour to a few centres.

2. "Development" became a new name for colonialism. Ireland as a nation began to develop a pathetic faith in the benevolence of powerful economies, relying on branches of multinational corporations to provide jobs. We failed to persuade many of these corporations to reduce their levels of profit repatriation

47

or to locate more of their core activities within Ireland. The official mind embraced the ideology of high technology of capital intensive programmes but little grasp of those criteria by which it might assess and control the performance of these new wonder programmes. Although the accumulated evidence shows that technology was as much part of the problem as of the answer, it was still projected as the panacea for a prosperous future.

3. The destruction of self-help and self-reliance—big organisations with a lot of public money were given the task of development. They depended heavily on that money and on public relations to promote industry, but failed completely to use the initiative of the people. Their terms of reference had very little to do with people at local level. They tended to monopolise development and create dependency.

Certainly, the social effects of the situation today have the horrific proportions of an epidemic.

The strategies pursued since 1970 have been a dismal failure on a number of fronts. A few interesting statistics about the employment situation tell us how ineffective these strategies have been.

- Between 1961 and 1991, the total increase in employment in Ireland was 61,000. Of that increase, the mid-west accounted for 0.5% or 337 extra jobs. The increase in the east was 110,000.

- Between 1985 and 1990, every region increased its employment or held its own—*except the mid-west, which suffered a decline of 0.8%*. In fact, through the 1980s, the numbers employed in the mid-west declined by 5,800. The people of Ireland are surely owed at least an unconditional apology from all those responsible for such an ineffective use, if not abuse, of power and an apology for the mind-management that has been taking place down through the years.

48

I have already referred to the fact that local resource development was regarded as amateur and second-rate, insignificant and not worthwhile. Such initiatives were not taken seriously and were left to voluntary groups. I have pointed to the sharp contrast in the treatment of our own and of those who come from abroad. Thus the self-esteem of many people—as individuals, as families, as communities—was eroded: they were not significant players in the development process. Government bodies and development agencies, who found no problem in attracting foreign industry with tens of thousands of pounds, found many obstacles to giving anything to local entrepreneurs.

While the Irish tax payer funded the industrial development effort, she/he is somehow deemed not quite good enough to participate in it in any other capacity.

The efforts of those who work at local development have attempted to redress that inequity. What have we found? We have found a resource of educated, intelligent, resourceful, imaginative, creative people. But these same positive people have been fed such an inedible diet of false promises, unachievable programmes and insurmountable barriers to self-help that they have rightly become cynical—at worst hopeless and, in most cases, stifled by lack of support and bureaucracy.

No one can seriously expect any person in this country to have faith in the continuance of such policies.

We have every right to say after 30 years: "Your strategies have not worked. Let's give some serious attention, serious commitment and serious funding to the only real alternative, apart from the emigrant ships and planes, namely the people themselves with all their human resources combined with local resources."

The Present

I am reasserting the *central role of people* in the development process. The innate intelligence, resourcefulness, imagination,

49

creativity, skills, heritage and personal commitment of the people must be seen as the primary asset in development.

Placing people at the centre of the development process, rather than seeing them as a factor of development—as in land, capital and labour—presupposes a radical shift in the approach to development. If people are the root of development, what is the task of those who are promoting it?

1. *The first task is that the support agencies remove themselves from the centre of the stage to a less visible role, and indeed some should be removed from the stage altogether.*

2. The second step demands that the agencies rethink their traditional interventions—from one of making people more receptive of development to one of helping them become the architects of it.

3. A third task is one of interacting with others involved in the development agenda, especially in education and training. In what way can schools and teachers reflect a more student-centred, people-centred emphasis? Schools have traditionally operated on the "jug and mug" principle, the student being the mug into which knowledge was poured from the jug. Such an approach has tended to ignore or even ridicule the vast array of non-intellectual talents a student may bring with him/her into the school. A people-centred development would suggest that these are precisely the talents which should be developed in schools.

The linking of native human resources with other local resources is the surest means of developing indigenous enterprises and of enabling local people to construct an acceptable living and enriching lifestyle. Most counties in Ireland are uniquely blessed with such resources, but we have a long way to go to realise them. For example, look at my native County Clare:

- It has more than 200 miles of coastline but a miniscule fishing or maritime industry.

- Average farm-size in Clare is larger than the average for practically every EC country except England. Yet Clare has severe agricultural income problems and a widespread pessimism prevails regarding the future of agriculture.

- One of our greatest resources is milk. It is worth £30m to the economy of Clare. Yet out of a total of 3,300 dairy farmers in 1984, about 1,000 have dropped out. Of the remainder, two-thirds are at risk of dropping out. However, realistic recommendations are now available which could halve the number of farm families dropping out of milk production. Nationally, this could mean the retention of 15,000 farm families on viable enterprises.

- Lough Derg is the biggest inland waterway in the Republic of Ireland.

- The Irish music and archaeological heritage of the county is unsurpassed.

- The environmental uniqueness of the Burren gives it a global significance.

In summary, my native county has a multitude of unique resources.

I am quite sure that the same applies to most other counties. With careful and enlightened approaches, they offer the potential not only for development but for a *different type of development*, one that is appropriate to the area, reflects the hearts and the minds of the people and does not hand over the county to multinational finance and its agents to be turned into a cultural and environmental Disneyland.

What Are We Doing?

My own involvement in local resource development goes back to 1972. In that year a few of us came together and founded an organisation called the Rural Resource Organisation. It emerged out of these basic perceptions:

- A dissatisfaction with the outcome of prevailing development strategies and a belief in a new strategy

- That strategy should be founded on principles of smallness, cooperation and resource development.

We felt that unless the disease of poverty was tackled at its source, in the rural areas, outside the big cities, it would continue to manifest itself in three ways: mass migration into cities, mass unemployment and mass dependency.

In 1983, we founded Rural Finance Limited and a Resource Centre in the same year. We managed to borrow money at low interest rates from different sources and invested that money in a number of projects throughout the country. We believed then—and we still believe—that major growth potential exists at local level if natural resources are developed to the full. The results of our efforts to date are that we have built approximately 2,500 houses, 120 communities in 13 counties. Through this effort, 10,000 people established homes in rural areas, many of them bringing their skills with them. They in turn set up little enterprises. In bringing back people in the 20/40 age group and young families, they in turn moved other things:

- Average village population increased by 30%.

- Rural schools expanded instead of closing.

- Community centres and village hotels were built.

- Small industries were generated, new shops opened.

- Emigrants returned to their home.

- Transport, water and sewerage services have improved.

- Other houses were built.

- Professional services have been provided—doctors, chemists, etc.

- Young farmers stayed on farms (when their own age group return).

- Spin-off investments have been estimated at three times the value of RRO housing developments.

We financed about 28 projects through Rural Finance and through the Resource Centre, identifying potential in a range of areas—forestry, alternative farming, tourism, etc.

This was done without any state support, either from regional or national authorities. Major obstacles had, in fact, to be overcome, such as the provision of basic services like water and sewerage and the maintenance of these for a long number of years.

The Future

The most significant development is the change in *attitude* towards development. This is already fully accepted in Europe, resulting in the establishment of the LEADER programme, a direct response from Brussels to the ineffective ways of tackling unemployment in peripheral regions.

Conscious of this new awakening in Europe, we developed Rural Resource Development Ltd.

Rural Resource Development Ltd

RRD is a partnership of organisations with a long established history of "bottom up" development activity. These are Rural Resource Organisation, Golden Vale, Teagasc, Clare Marts and community-based organisations. It also integrates the activities of a wide variety of organisations such as FÁS, CERT, and the VEC. It has also pulled together people from the world of industry, funding and so on. Effectively, it represents a unique attempt at the integration of all the significant actors in the rural development endeavour, providing in its structure and philosophy an unqualified commitment to the "bottom up" approach.

This has taken place under the new EC LEADER Initiative, from which funding is provided for groups such as this: those who join together for the purpose of drawing up and implementing business plans for their areas.

The LEADER Initiative emphasises certain necessary features:

- The group should have a real local presence.
- It should be representative of the community.
- It should be able to demonstrate its solvency, its administrative expertise and its ability to carry out its plan it puts together.

At RRD we have developed two broad programme areas:

(1) Development promotion

(2) Development support.

Development Promotion
In this programme, we are launching four separate initiatives in a promotional role in the areas of

(a) community training and education

(b) school-based enterprise programme

(c) the establishment of an Investment Fund for local enterprise

(d) networking.

For example, we maintain that there are major implications for schools in a post-industrial world. To quote one of our greatest literary figures: "All's changed, changed utterly." Our education system has so far failed to make the kinds of adjustments essential to meeting the actual needs of post-industrial society. Between 1971 and 1986, the number of accountants trebled and the numbers of auctioneers and lawyers doubled. In contrast, the numbers of engineers increased by less than 50%.

Development Support
The main thrust of RRD's programme in this area is to match development culture with development opportunity. We feel that the most effective role we can play is to establish development programmes which will provide a welcoming environment for

individual projects, where such projects are organically linked into an overall strategy for the sector.

On the basis of 200 project proposals received to date, seven broad sectoral strategies are being developed:

- Agriculture and Supplementary Enterprises (with emphasis on family farms)
- Mariculture and Fisheries
- Small Industry (with emphasis on food, timber and fish processing
- Tourism
- Crafts
- Culture
- Community Initiatives

All project developments are supported by training, advisory, marketing and funding strategies.

Each sectoral strategy provides a comprehensive framework within which the individual projects can be developed in a systematic, interlinked and reasonably secure way.

Conclusion

If the past has led to an erosion of the belief of the people in themselves, there is at last recognition that a radical new approach is needed. Sustainable developments in the productive sectors of the economy must be rooted in the people and their resources.

This time round, the trust must swing back to the people and away from the agencies, the verbalisers and the globe-trotters. Local structures involving local people and doers, with the back-up of schools and banks, and administered by a few committed people, seem to be the way forward.

It is a time to stop tinkering around with the old policies and promises of employment with strategies that don't and can't work.

The structure now in place in County Clare is an interesting approach. The forces of education and training, agriculture and industry are prepared to combine with an organisation which has played a pioneering role in the development of rural Ireland. All of these are now combining to work with the people. It is experimental, as yet operating only on a pilot basis, but I see a huge future for it. It could be the way forward.

The clear message is that power must return to the people. This must begin by raising consciousness and enabling people to reflect on the situation before acting. The process then is one of reflection upon one's world and of acting upon it to change it.

And so the task of empowerment begins not with structures but with education. We are now realising that the structures of decision-making have been dominated by a few economists, administrators and politicians. They dictated what kind of society we would have, without any participatory role for the people.

Furthermore, they promised a utopia to individuals, families and communities based on economics, as if people never mattered. This was a total contradiction. It was an approach at building a society without ethics, morality, truth, spirituality.

The technocrats and the politicians speak a language which belongs to a defunct industrial society. The people belong to another world, a post industrial culture. The key demands of this culture lie in the areas of participation, ethics and spirituality.

Let us now go on to emphasise how important it is to find a way forward which focuses on families and communities.

6. Giving Power To The People

The thoughts put forward in this book spring from the experience of acting with local people. It must be said, however, that this country has gone too far in substituting the Conference/Seminar/Verbalising industry, followed by reports, for action. There are too many who believe that, if they give a lecture about something, they are really doing something to solve the problem. This applies in a very real sense to the world of development and those to whom it really belongs.

There are many reports sitting on library shelves whose messages are anything but dull. They record major landmarks that the Republic of Ireland has passed since 1960 on its road to the high consumption society.

1966: For the first time since the great famine of the 1840s, *a rise in population is recorded.*

1969: The value of our *industrial* exports exceeds that of our *agricultural* exports for the first time.

1971: The census of this year records that, again for the first time, *the proportion of the population living in urban areas is greater than that living in rural areas.*

1978: The World Bank produces its first ever report on the world economy. In a ranking of 125 countries, Ireland is placed inside the elite group of 30 industrialised countries.

1979:   The census in April of this year reveals that *the number of young people aged 15-24 has grown by one half* (five more for every 10 so aged in 1961).

Such landmarks since then are more than easy to find. The landmark provided by the World Bank in 1978 is an example of how we are no longer considered *a sean bhean bhocht* by the rest of the world.

The terms used to describe the social and economic changes that Ireland experienced in the '60s and '70s were *industrialisation* and *urbanisation*, twin processes whereby a society comes to depend more on factories than on farms for wealth and jobs, and on cities rather than the countryside as the places where most of its people live. These movements which began in the late 1950s make 1958 probably a more important date than 1916 for understanding the society we are living in now. Ireland then passed some kind of turning point.

When over 400,000 people left Ireland in the 1950s, it was clear that some change *had* to be made. Abandoned country houses and bolted-up dwellings were multiplying everywhere. A new strategy for providing jobs was designed. It was accepted that agriculture would continue to make many people redundant. The best source of new jobs was identified as industry—a particular type of industry. The rest of Europe had recovered from the war and was beginning to enjoy higher living standards all round. Ireland would get more jobs and factories making the sort of things that these more affluent societies overseas would buy. This meant exporting. An elaborate and generous syste of aids and incentives was built up by the Irish state for the industrialist who would export. American, British, German, Dutch and Japanese companies availed of these incentives.

By 1981, foreign-owned firms were employing 80,000 people in Ireland, some 34% of the manufacturing workforce. They brought a fresh dynamism to the Irish economy. A battery of development agencies was established to promote and support them. These companies did not sail into our seas unannounced and free. For example, the Irish state spent some £2 billion on industrial policy in the nine years 1973 to 1981.

In short then, the new workbenches generated more private wealth than the old, but cost a lot of public money to provide and maintain.

Redistribution

Ireland has thus been a market economy for a long number of years. We generate more wealth than ever, but actively involve only one-third of the population in doing so. That presents us with a very basic challenge: how to ensure that the unemployed and the unemployable somehow get in on the act. How are the jobless two-thirds to get access to the wealth which the employed third is generating?

There has been progress. All our young people, the elderly, the disabled, mothers minding children, the unemployed and the unemployable, are being better supported today than in the past. Instances of nineteenth century poverty such as malnutrition, illiteracy, squatted housing, etc., are becoming rarer, although pockets of such destitution still remain. In short, the state is softening the harshness of the market economy.

We began to believe that poverty had become a marginal phenomenon, limited to exceptional cases which could easily be taken care of by relief measures. But, in fact, what had happened over the last number of years was that this approach made poverty invisible. It no longer belonged in the welfare society. There was no political majority to form an actual struggle against poverty. It came to be understood as more or less the fault of the poor person alone.

It became clear also that the oil crisis of the '70s abruptly changed the social and political climate in Ireland and indeed in western Europe. Many people viewed the cost of social relief programmes as one of the most serious obstacles to pulling out of the economic recession. This led to a policy of subsidies to stimulate profits from trade and industry, and the privatisation of more and more state-run business. The free enterprise system was encouraged as the engine of society, and the social system was seen as secondary.

We now have a serious disparity between rich and poor in both material and social psychological terms in Ireland. A large section of Irish society has now ended up in the ghetto. The state is in danger of splitting, with the majority using almost any available means to maintain and expand its existing privileges and security, and a powerless minority with no opportunity to advance its interest.

Solidarity

The number of marginalised people in Ireland has grown dramatically over the last decade. The state now not only maintains and expands privileges and security for one section of society but it has actually ceased to locate many of its services in broken rural and urban communities. *The marginalised are serviced from a distance*. The gardai, the medics and financial services are no longer located in the broken communities, rural or urban. They are no longer engaged with the people, involved in their social activities: they come as authority figures, not as friends, not as supports, not as acquaintances.

The nature of our policies in the last three decades has led to a very divided society, one that has been hidden. The Ireland of the rich is well known. Our tour guides and ambassadors are happy to sell it, and our government strives to project that image. The Ireland of banks, industries, technology and development assistance, the Ireland of generous campaigns against hunger in other parts of the world—this Ireland is well publicised. The other side of Ireland is forgotten and suppressed.

Our economic system is organised to favour the strong. This means, in effect, that the support for those who are marginalised tends to come from a distance, with a notable absence of solidarity. This is an alarming development. It is not accidental—it is supported and directed by powerful institutions in society. The organisation of our economy in this way has led to serious poverty and unemployment, but it has also led to the breakdown of justice, of solidarity, of spirituality, and to a serious breakdown of trust.

At the very time when a dual society threatens to develop in Ireland as in western Europe, the question of *location* is of vital importance. If society splits into two groups, where then are our teachers, our doctors and our gardai located? We can all put on the brakes, give a shout, throw things out the open window for those left behind on the station—but will we also get off the train and remain with those left behind?

I speak for a lot of rural communities and indeed for some urban communities, when I say that I am deeply conscious of the absence of a lot of people who give service to the community. The transformation of the poor or welfare victims from *subjects* of charity or welfare to *objects* has far-reaching consequences. It has consequences for engagement itself, which must rid itself of all condescension and must stand in solidarity, sometimes at a price. It has political consequences: no more operating from a power base at the centre of things in order to accumulate more power (to improve the situation of the few) but rather to help the powerless to develop their power. Even those in secure jobs in banks, in semi-state enterprises, in the civil and local government, are beginning to distrust direction from their own power bases at the centre.

It is quite clear that this situation must be tackled as a matter of urgency. I believe it can be tackled by a radical change in development policy, one which will include radical change on the part of people who offer service.

Development

Before the divisions between the powerful and the poor become too wide, we must face up to the realities of our system and acknowledge that the strategies for economic growth and a

61

balanced spread of benefits have very obviously not worked. One of the reasons is the refusal of those who put those policies and strategies together to acknowledge that they have not worked. Such an admission would be to confess failure.

We now badly need a switch of focus which will give serious attention, serious commitment and serious funding to the only live option open to us apart from the emigrant ships and planes— *that option is people.*

Not very long ago, a business conference in Limerick heard Detta O'Catháin point out that, year after year, annual reports of development agencies and companies keep on coming out with the well-worn cliché about people being the greatest resource of a firm or of a nation. Yet, those same companies, public and private, put more money and time into planning the next office block or piece of equipment than developing the vast skills and creative talents of what they keep saying is their greatest resource.

We have politicians going on about our "brightest and best", but failing to take a radical look at how we have failed in job creation in this country and failed to look for an alternative based on people. And we have the constant reminders of how important people are—while we pull away the medical service, shut down the post offices and reduce postal deliveries, close schools and withdraw the reassuring garda presence from many of our streets.

People are not only our greatest resource, but combine into an irresistible power which may explain why the dormant power of people is resisted and denied. There is a conscious and deliberate effort, going on for a long time, not to give power to large numbers of intelligent, creative people. The few who have power are afraid of losing it. There is no doubt in my mind that the creativity of people is our only sure path to avoiding a disaster which growing unemployment will surely bring. That creativity is stifled and starved of resources, of funding and of various kinds of service back-ups. I have learned this from my experience over the past 20 years working in rural and urban communities.

A substantial reduction in unemployment is not an impossible goal provided every sector of Irish society stands solidly with the creative, talented people and their resources. This includes gardai, bankers, teachers, doctors and other professionals, many of whom now serve communities from a distance. This has eroded the people's self-esteem and their belief in their own capacity for action—the belief that they can play a significant role in the development process.

All across Ireland, people are now at last believing in themselves, only because they cannot get jobs here and they cannot easily go abroad. They realise that the policies of yester-year have failed. There is a whole new energy being unleashed; projects like LEADER are of fundamental value. In the light of the conviction that integrated community is vital at local level before it can become a reality at European level, it is a time for all services to be re-examined and re-directed.

Where do we find hope in the Ireland of the future? Almost certainly where we are, locally. We must return to it, so let's conclude with some of the people and places where hope is to be found.

7. Hope In A Changing Ireland

"It will be the first time in my life I will have to live alone but I have great neighbours." That is what an elderly widow said to me recently at the wedding of her last child. She was sad but the neighbours were her great hope. And she said: "I'm good to pray."

A young woman, mother of four children, whose husband had died suddenly a few days before, told me: "We are holding up because we can talk to one another but I feel bitter because he was taken so young—we had 18 wonderful years together, and so I will have the memories; so many couples are unhappy."

They are just two experiences I had in the space of a couple of days. I could talk about others—to do with loneliness, with the pain of unemployment, with the sadness of losing a child, with the awful hurt of marriage breakdown.

Where do we find hope in the midst of pain? These women told me they will find it in the neighbours, in the family, in sharing and supporting, in trusting God, in praying a lot, giving Him time.

Finding hope in modern Ireland can be difficult. News headlines seem always full of bad news—crime, unemployment, family breakdown. It would be easy to get depressed.

But there are real signs that things are changing again. And this time the change is coming from the bottom rather than from the top. Those who have been living with realities on the ground are discovering again that if we live apart from God and people, we are living an impoverished life. If our contact with the world is through some sections of the national media and if the topics of our own discussions come from the latest headline then we have been removing ourselves from neighbours, family and indeed from God.

Life can be very full and enriching when we return to the ground and we are in contact with, for example, old people and rediscover their wisdom, the gift of faith and the value of prayer. When we meet married couples who are working hard at living up to their promises, then we discover that marriage has a relevance, that breakdown is not as widespread as we are led to believe and we rediscover a wonderful witness in fidelity—that same witness that is evident in the lives of many priests and religious. When we meet young people who are open and honest, who are prepared to take risks, who see the world as their stage but value home, the place they come from, we are challenged and we realise that we have nothing to fear in handing this society over to a new generation. When we meet sick people, we discover how much growth and life there is in pain: the meaning of carrying the cross with patience comes home to us.

Thank God there are signs we have very definitely entered a new era which brings great hope. We must acknowledge these. People are rediscovering their God, their neighbour, themselves. But there are great challenges too—for the church, for political, professional, business and other vested interests. The challenge seems to be taking the form of: "Listen to the people, hear what they are saying and respond. It won't be easy, because you will have to let go of power and wealth, both of which have blinded us."

St. Paul's words to the Ephesians are making a lot of sense in our time: "I want to urge you in the name of the Lord, not to go on living aimless lives … You must give up your old way of life … Your mind must be renewed by a spiritual revolution."

Are their signs that the seeds of this quiet revolution are being sown in Ireland today by the hidden people?

Change

There is no doubt that Ireland changed radically somewhere around the early 1960s. There is no doubt either that in general terms the present generation of Irish people is better fed, clothed, housed and schooled than any previous generation.

On the other hand, we are living under such a cloud of instability as was never experienced by any previous generation— instability in the plague of unemployment, instability in family life, instability brought about by false promises, the over-use of public relations that created unreal expectations.

The roots of the most fundamental change ever experienced in this country go back to the early 1960s and to the promises of new freedoms. We all wanted to be free, but did we want to take responsibilities for these freedoms? Certainly new forms of slavery have appeared. Is it because we tried to build a society without God? Is it because we became so preoccupied with ourselves that we became isolated from our neighbours? Is it because we so foolishly believed that a consumer society could satisfy the hunger of the heart and the spirit?

Are we beginning to realise that we made serious mistakes, and at great cost to ourselves? On a daily basis, our headlines are screaming stark warnings at us—warnings which clearly spell out that there is no such thing as a free economy. Otherwise, business will be carried out in the name of self-interest. Justice and law and conscience will be seriously violated. We have warnings about unbridled freedoms which have led young people to cry for help. People in broken communities, urban and rural, are warning that they are not impressed with empty words, false promises and cynical schemes.

In focusing so heavily on material possessions, we begin to lose a sense of God; eventually we lose a sense of sin. Many of our social problems stem from the fact that there has been a widespread distrust of anyone who used the word "sin" or the word "moral"—almost as if they were out of date. These have been costly mistakes and our business, family and community life have suffered.

Hope

There are real signs, however, that we are beginning to identify priorities again. There is a real search going on which is taking the form of deepening our relationships with God, with family and determining our economic future within ourselves, our own resources, our own communities. We have entered a new era: like all resurrections, the hope for the future is coming from the bottom rather than the top. We have a vital, thinking, enterprising people emerging from the hidden Ireland. When things are at their worst, people on the ground dig deep because they live with realities. And when things are creaking at the top, you will always find a return to the ordinary people on the ground.

There is nothing new in this, of course. Christianity emerged from the fringes. It was to the outcasts, the sick, the poor and the disenfranchised that Christ addressed himself. It was from such unlikely soil that the seed of Christianity blossomed. In such soil also lies hope for the future in Ireland.

We are once again recognising the need for a spiritual dimension. We are embedding ourselves in our Celtic origins and our traditions. There is a renewed interest in traditional Irish society and this is finding new ways of expressing itself in prayer but also in music, literature, drama, craftwork and art.

Challenges

Prayer
There are challenges for the church. By "church", I mean *us, God's people, pobal Dé, pilgrim people*. We need to give time and space to bow our heads and bend our knees and be in touch with the mystery of God. It is there we will be empowered to dig deep, to commit ourselves seriously to one another in determining

67

our future. We need to pray more. Many of us need help to discover new ways of praying.

In a busy noisy world, we need solitude, to be alone with God. There is a discipline we need to impose on ourselves, on a daily basis, if this is to happen. To discover how spiritual renewal is brought about is the major need of our time. There is great hope in the fact that growing numbers are aware of this. Our liturgies, our lives, will only find meaning when they are rooted in solid private prayer. We need to make a new start and ensure that each day we have an appointment with God. I think we have realised again that:

> If our lives have been too busy to pray, then we are much busier than God wants us to be.

A New Europe

Another great sign of hope and a challenge for all of us is that we are now part of a new Europe. For example, the links between us, one of the smallest, and a country like Germany, by far the most powerful, are growing steadily. In general more and more Europeans are coming to Ireland.

The movement has been in the other direction as well. Thousands of young, well-educated Irish men and women are finding permanent or temporary work in offices, factories and small businesses throughout Europe. This is a time of opportunity for those who did not have it at home, not only to find work but to work and develop on a wider stage with its mix of language, culture and values.

It is also time for us to strengthen and deepen our sense of place, at home. The emergence of local radio, community groups, the interest in developing our talents at local level are all a sign of hope. There will be no integrated European Community unless there are integrated local communities at home.

There is a major challenge here to political and business interests and to development agencies. The challenge is to review their position of monopoly, dominance and power, and to admit they have made serious mistakes, to allow people take control of their own lives. This is the way the EC wants it. It is what the people want, as expressed by them through the initiative of the western bishops and many other grass-roots movements taking place in Ireland today.

We have much to offer Europe. Our Christian heritage and tradition, our deep sense of God and neighbour, our willingness to work together—these are the strengths we bring to a renewed spirit of mission in Europe.

Faith and Justice

Another great sign of hope is that we are beginning to rediscover once again the link between faith and justice. The Church is re-emerging as the outspoken champion of the rights of the poor. Church people—cleric, religious and lay—stand solidly with people in broken rural and urban communities, at a time when public service people no longer live among them but offer their service only from a distance. Standing solidly with broken people and broken communities is a significant witness and, in many ways, is what the Church of Christ is all about. It demands courage. It is one of the great challenges of our day. It is a great sign of hope that men and women who never make headlines, silent people who are rich in interior life, stand solidly with the broken and with the poor. They must be affirmed and encouraged. "Respectability" must be defined in this form of service.

Our hope for the future lies in rediscovering our roots—our sense of God, our need to give Him back the time He has given to us. It lies in rediscovering our sense of place and neighbour and family in that place and ensuring that they be given time for talking, listening, sharing. It lies in returning to a '90s version of *meitheal* and *muintearas*, so that together we can create a livelihood and a community spirit for our own and our neighbour's children. The hidden Ireland has a rich culture; our traditions are strong; we have vast natural resources. It only requires continuing to develop what has now begun with our gifts, our talents,

69

creativity and vision. It is in this movement that we will restore peace, a sense of trust and loyalty to Ireland and make a vital contribution to Europe.

Conclusion

We are now part of a Europe which calls itself a *community*. It is acknowledged that there can be no European integration without a strong sense of community which, indeed, must include *a sense of spirituality*. It is further acknowledged that there can be no European integration without local integration. Herein lies the great challenge.

The Europe of economics existed for 35 years. That Europe has now turned again to a political integration. How is this possible if politics is in a state of crisis? Politicians and government development agencies are continuing to speak an economic language that is out-dated. For example, they continue to refer to *jobs they created. They didn't, they don't and they never will create these jobs.* The people want an environment in which to create their own. That is the role of government.

People have changed and the culture of which they are part has changed. We live in a post-industrial, post-urban society. People want to participate in determining their own future. They want localised structures. There is an obvious hunger for *meaning*— to life, to politics and economics. They want honesty and truth.

So there is an enormous challenge here for leaders of member states of the EC. It is no longer good enough for a political leader to dangle financial carrots of billions of pounds before the citizens of a country like Ireland. This merely deepens the cynicism. People want much more—they want to participate. They want to be contributors as well as being beneficiaries.

They also want meaning, and here the churches are challenged. They must speak out and spell out that *a Europe without a soul is dead.*They must do this in a language that people understand.

There has never been a time in any society, in any part of the world, which did not produce people prepared to challenge

70

materialism and plead for a different order of priorities. The thoughts in this book are put together in order to try to generate debate on these priorities. It is suggested that we should—indeed we must—give serious thought again to the family and community as the basis of a development strategy for the future.

It is further suggested that there is one truth and we must return to a profound respect for truth. The language challenging materialism has differed down the years. Yet the message is always the same:

> "Seek ye *first* the kingdom of God and **all these things** (the material things which we also need) will be *added* unto you."

Today this message reaches us not only from wise people and prophets but from the course of events. There are many danger signals. These events speak to us in the language of terrorism, breakdown, unemployment, pollution and exhaustion. It is becoming apparent that there is now a real threat that **all these things** [promised by Christ] will not be available to a lot of people unless we put first things first.

We cannot continue to shrink away from the truth. In our Christian tradition, the truth is now too often stated in a language that has lost meaning for many who travel in the fast lane. Maybe we should return to a language which centres on the great virtues of *prudence, justice, fortitude* and *temperance*.

We must seek and find alternatives which are practical. I hope this book can make some contribution to a badly needed debate.

Father Harry Bohan

Father Harry Bohan was born in 1938 in Feakle, Co. Clare. He was educated at the local National School, at St. Flannan's College, Ennis, and at Maynooth, where he was ordained in 1963. At Maynooth he took a keen interest in rural sociology, studying under Dr. Newman. He continued his sociological studies at the University of South Wales, Cardiff, where he obtained an M.Sc.Econ. The subject of his thesis was "The Effects of Industrialisation on the Settlement Pattern of Britain".

Before he returned to Ireland in 1968, he worked with Irish emigrants in Birmingham.

To counter the emigration pattern which industrialisation was imposing on rural communities, he founded in 1972 the Rural Housing Organisation. Its activities have brought 2,500 families back to 120 small communities throughout the west of Ireland.

In 1983, Rural Resource Organisation (formerly RHO) expanded its activities to embrace not only housing but also the wider aspects of rural resource development. To promote this second objective, it established two additional components to its activities, namely Rural Finance and Rural Resource Centre.

Rural Finance was established with a view to retaining capital in rural areas and attracting finance from individuals and companies at reduced interest rates.

The Resource Centre was established with a view to assisting community organisations to tackle local unemployment. RRO is now a partnership of organisations—together they form Rural Resource Development (EC initiative in Co. Clare).

Father Bohan is deeply involved in pastoral work, and has directed many diocesan retreats.

A keen sportsman, he managed the Clare hurling team which won National League titles in 1977 and 1978.

Father Bohan has written extensively on the subject of Christianity and economic development, and has broadcast often on radio and television. He is the author of *Ireland Green* (1979) and *Roots in a Changing Society* (1982).

Father Harry Bohan is a priest of the Killaloe diocese and is based in Shannon, Co. Clare.